A Unique P.O.V. (Point of View)

Patty Candil

BookLeaf Publishing

Presentation by *BookLeaf Publishing*

Web: www.bookleafpub.com

E-mail: info@bookleafpub.com

ISBN: 9789357214421

First edition 2022

For my husband, I whale you infinity.

For my dad, thank you for raising me.

ACKNOWLEDGEMENT

I wrote this book not knowing what the daily challenges would be, but with some convincing from my husband, I kept on. It's not the emotions that are hard but knowing when to put the pen down. I would first like to thank my husband, Brendon L. L'Heureux, for believing in me and my capabilities. Thank you for listening to every poem, every edit and revision, and for pushing upwards and onwards. Thank you to my best friend, Abigail Yarbrough Helms, for being there when I'd cry when I wrote and giving me hope that I'd find a true love who'd also listen to my poems. A big thank you to my father, Anthony J. Candil, who instituted me a fondness for reading and writing and believed in my dreams of becoming a writer. A sarcastic thanks to my biological father, my mother, my siblings, and those who have hurt me, by giving me material to write about. I couldn't have done it without you! To Ms. Jevon Westmoreland, thank you for pushing me into my writing minor, reviewing and giving me feedback on my poetry, and making me believe that I have what it takes to become published. To Mr. James Taylor, thank you for confiding in me, and showing me how my poetry can help shed a light on mental health, and bring people together. Thank you to the poets and writers that inspired me to begin writing, especially Sabrina Benaim, Reuben Holmes (r.h. Sin), and William Shakespeare. And finally, thank you to Book Leaf Publishing for creating this December Writing Challenge and publishing my book.

PREFACE

The origin of A Unique P.O.V. begins in Madrid, Spain. I was born on Friday, November 13, 1998, supposedly the unluckiest day of the year. After I turned nine, my mother remarried, and my family and I moved to Texas. But it was in those first nine years that I experienced some of the worst moments of my life, moments that I still struggle to think about or write my emotions. The trauma caused by my biological father is something I wouldn't wish on my worst enemy because no child should ever have to go through that. But the trauma didn't stop once we moved to the United States because trauma follows you. Once I got to middle school, I began having night terrors. I was waking up in the middle of the night feeling like I couldn't breathe and had a terrifying sense of panic. That's when I started researching mental health at the school library, which there wasn't much information on since you're still a child, and children aren't supposed to worry about those things. I also experienced bullying at its finest. A boy who yelled at me in science class to go back to where I came from. A teacher would make comments and lower my grades', precisely because I'm from Spain. Other kids would pretend to be my friend to laugh in my face or use the information against me. That's when I started to write poetry, to have a way to express my feelings since my family wasn't one to talk about feelings unless they were "good" feelings. So by the time I got to high school, I was dealing with depression, anxiety, insomnia from the night terrors, a terrible relationship with food, etc. Even so, I had the school library. I researched articles, read books on mental health, and broadened my knowledge of my poetry. I came to find out that while many fiction books speak of depression and anxious feelings, those that touch on personality disorders tend to be extremists in their writing. Then the day before my junior year started, my boyfriend killed himself after almost being together for two years. My world shattered. I became an emotional zombie, numb. I got into an emotionally abusive relationship simply because they coaxed me into believing I would feel better. But alas, after a month of bleakness, I ended up in a mental hospital. In less than a month, I was diagnosed with Borderline Personality Disorder, Major Depression, Insomnia, and General Anxiety.

Once I arrived home, I felt like I was in prison. My birthday that year enclosed gas station cheese fries and singing myself a silent happy birthday while my parents watched TV. It took nine months before I went back to school and was able to contact my friends. And with much effort, I managed to finish school the same as them and walk the walk for my diploma. The real challenge had come, finding a university. How much distance could I put between myself and my controlling mother? The answer is 46 miles. I went to a Baptist university, where I forcibly took religious classes I loathed, became the victim of sexual harassment by a teacher, and met my favorite two teachers; Ms. Westmoreland, and Mr. Taylor. Thanks to those two teachers, I became confident in my writing, knowing that it would help others understand life from a mental health perspective. In 2020, right before Covid, I met my now husband. We knew each other and dated for three months before we got married, and we moved to Missouri right after due to his orders from the Army. The thing is, I didn't tell any of my family that I was going to get married, and they hadn't even met him yet. I gave them a chance, but due to how they had treated me my entire life, how they were treating me now, and how they spoke of my husband, I burned the bridge between myself and my family besides my dad (my stepfather). Since then, I haven't been happier and more stable. I wrote because I was sad and had no hope, but now I write because even though I might get sad, I have hope, belief, and people that love me unconditionally. Now on to the book. Please enjoy it, and I hope it brings you a new perspective.

My Borderline Personality Disorder

I live on Gray Street.
Between White Cove,
And Black Drive.
The tectonic plates of my body split like oil and water.

My irrational calmness and rational panic,
Battle for control over my tongue and the chambers of my heart.
My attached abandonment,
My premeditated impulsivity,
My fulfilling emptiness,
My stable identity crisis,
My brave paranoia,
My happy depression,
My calm anxiety,
And my healing trauma,
These are all symptoms of my Borderline Personality Disorder.
These are the makers that assemble my perspective.

Freedom

A breath of fresh air,
A weight off your shoulders,
A bird.
All expressions of freedom.

But no one tells you that the recalcitrance
feeling of freedom is fleeing.
Soon after the panic sets in,
You watch over your shoulder,
Wait impatiently for the other shoe to drop,
And if it doesn't drop, you self-sabotage.

We drown in the anxiety that that freedom we
fought so hard for,
is going to be taken from us once again.

Everyone talks about how good freedom feels,
But no one talks about the fact that we're just
going from one cage to another,
In an endless charade for a breath of fresh air
again.

My Name is Depression

I am the rain,
I am the crash,
And the bang.
I am everywhere.
I am the broken glass.
A lost picture,
A person that now,
Only live in your mind.
I am the forgotten,
And the lost,
But never found.
I am the darkness,
I am the winter,
I am the cold,
I am the hatred,
And the alone.
I am the tree branch that fell,
A black sheep in the crowd.
A lost locket,
In the ocean underground.
I am the goodbyes,
And broken hearts.
A fallen coffee cup,
And the tears on the ground.
I am the would-have-been,

Could have been,
But never was.
I am the drying paint.
The tunnel with no end,
A song with no sound,
And a book with no words.
I am the nightmare,
I am the emptiness.
The screaming silence,
And the silent scream.
I am the rain,
As it hits with a crash,
And it breaks with a bang.
I am always there.

Cutting You Off

I broke the binds that bonded me to you.
I burned the bridge of our relationship.
Your bullying and abuse sharpened my edges to a point.
My need to please you and be worthy of your love,
Made me compliant to toxic and unhealthy relationships.
My behavior and personality are the consequence of your words and actions.
If you call me manipulative or selfish,
It is only a reflection of you.

I am kind today because of me.
I am confident and compassionate because of the work that I put into myself.
I am worthy of being loved as I am,
No if's or buts.
It was never me that was the problem,
It was you.
And thanks to the sharpened edges you created,
I cut myself away from you.
Now I am free to thrive.
I am free to be happy without guilt.

Oblivion

We were told
Since we were young
To stay in the house
And do work
To keep our mouths shut
If we were hit or spat at
We were told that we were evil
That we were crazy
But yet they told us to act a certain way
Be a certain way
That if we didn't then we would be the outcast
The bystander
The odd one
We were told since we were young
To get good grades
To play this sport
And be in that club
That in order to get accepted we needed to have good grades
Be thin
Be pretty
Be sensible but not too much
We were told since we were young
Who to love
What to believe

And who to believe in
We were forced a sense of right and wrong that strangled any possibility of change
We were told what to be
Our future
And how to get there
Without even knowing if we'd have food the next day
We were told since we were young
You can change the world
Be different
Be kind
Be sweet
Be nice
Be courageous
Be the best you can be
But yet here we are
Afraid of being who we want to be to satisfy those who want us to be something we are not
Afraid to love
Afraid to be
Yet not afraid to put a gun against our head with the intention of death because society has made us this way
Is this what you pictured as parents
When you were raising your kids?

A Simple Question

If food is love,
Why are there people starving?

Finding Love

Growing up, I thought I knew what true love was.
I dreamed of meeting them at a concert, a bookshop, a cooking class, or school.
But I didn't. Instead, I found it in the watercolors of life.
I found love on the spider web of social media.
I found it smiling at me through lead drawings.
I found it walking in the park, asking for directions.
I found it at a bus stop complimenting my shirt.
And I found it singing karaoke in a bar.
I could never learn my lesson.
So after endlessly picking up the pieces and putting myself back together, I created titanium armor around myself.
I swore off love and welcomed my loneliness.
I played sad music through my sleepless nights as the salt-soaked pages soothed the unseen ruptures of my body.
Then at a soiree with friends, I met your smile.
I knew then I hadn't just met true love but that they would be with me till death do us part.
And so far, it has.

Forgetting to Prevent

Do you ever wish you could go back and erase a few lines, paragraphs, pages, or chapters of your story?
I used to.
I used to wish the abuse hadn't happened, my heart hadn't broken, and I had a stable, happy family.
I used to wish I had a stress-free childhood, I could achieve any dream, no matter how hard or complicated, and my verisimilitude happiness was real.

I tried to eradicate my memories with alcohol-dripping lips and smokey lungs.
I looked for my prince charming-the one who could help me forget- under the covers of meaningless sex.
I wrote until my fingers bled and my hands cramped, trying to get the flashbacks out of my system.
I prayed to whoever had created me to tell me where to go and when, so I could die naturally soon.

I used to wish I could forget what made me, me.

Until I realized I could stop others from making the same mistakes I did,
That I am the only one who can prevent someone else from feeling this way,
That I am the only one who can avert another me.

Seeking Comfort in a Friend

Come.
Sit beside me,
And lay your tired head on my lap.

Allow my hands to brush the tangles from your hair,
Easing your worries and your pain.
Let yesterday's sadness stand idle by the door,
Accompanied by tomorrow's anxieties.

Permit your heavy eyelids to close,
Rest in the peaceful thought that you are protected.

Grant your mind permission to dream once again,
Knowing that I will be here to guard you and keep you embraced.

The Dragon

Hello... But when I say hello, I really mean, I love you. But when I say I love you, I mean your laughter is a sun cascading sparks into my belly, where a fire-breathing dragon waits impatiently for more. I mean, I am a hoard of lost and found objects. I mean the walls around me are 6-inch steel, you know? When I say I hoard, I mean pieces of string, and buttons, buttons everywhere; I am a walking pandemonium. I mean you walked into my life seeing the shiny silver stars under my eyes, and the lost golden ring with three pearls my mother gave me. I mean I lose memories more often than I lose my phone, and I find in others' memories they dug 6 feet underground. I mean, I am a shovel that never stops digging myself into a hole. I mean, silver spoon fed with tainted silverware. I mean, I created a dragon of broken things that you sparked back to life. So when I really mean I love you, I'm only saying, hello.

Stuck on You

I was right in a way
I'm the only one to blame
I came back, and we tried again.
But here I am
Broken like a clock
Whose only right twice a day.
I visited you and fell for you as if it'd just been yesterday that you touched my soul.
You promised we'd try again
You promised you'd put in 100%
You promised
You promised
Well, you broke that promise.
You know what you were doing
You know how to get back into my heart
You knew the words to say and how to take my breath away.
You played me like a chess piece
You played with my heart like a tambourine
Intertwined your fingers with mine
Only to stab me in the back with your other hand.
You told me you still love me
Why haven't you proved it?

Why does it feel like I'm screaming at you, but you can't hear me?
You say you're sorry for the pain
But you push the knife further up anyway
I'm staring you in the eyes, begging you to please,
Please don't do this again
You say you'll call
You say you'll text
And I understand you're busy
But give me a sign that you care.
I am stuck on you
A piece of gum on your shoe
I'm crying in public because of you
And there is nothing I can do.

Acceptance

When you're laughing until you're choking
You can easily swear
That you will wake up
Every day for the rest of your days

But when you're drowning in your tears
And the walls are closing in
You promise to every existing God
That you won't make it again

The days are bright and shiny
Fake smiles everywhere
Everyone thinks your life is perfect
And so do you of them

We wear our smiles so naturally
That it's almost hard to tell
How broken and sad we are
Until we are alone by ourselves

We open every scar we have
From the ones in our arms to the ones eating up
our hearts
We let it happen over and over again
To feel something different from despair

We go nights without sleeping
Because we're sure nobody is there
We've fooled ourselves into believing
"Hell, I'm a mess no one can help"

But we're so wrong in every aspect
No one is too far gone for no one to care
We tell others to find the light at the end of the tunnel
Or that if everything's not alright then it's not the end

That's right, but not correct
Because this is life
Not some monopoly play
Where you can make money, pay debts, and win the game

In life, not everything is okay
There's not always light
And you are by yourself
But you learn to live that way and accept the good and the bad because we're all we have left

Many call this acceptance
Others call it survival
I call it as I see it
Managing life as I live it

The Lucky One

In a world where healthy relationships are
expected and wanted but not granted,
I want to brag about my husband.

Fate hadn't played her last card.
She kept the pages blank.
Hoping we'd find each other
Before the clock struck twelve

It took heartbreak to find him.
Hidden in the watercolors of life
I'd sworn off love after a shattered heart
Yet he painted me a finer one

The night we met, I slapped him on a dare.
Yet ended the night snuggled on our friend's
green couch.
Within a week, I was meeting his friends.
Within three months' our vows were spoken
lakeside.

He balances the seesaw that is my mentality,
And sponges my emotions,
Soothing them efficaciously.

He surprises me with themed dates,
Lady and the Tramp tablecloth and spaghetti
included.
He cares for me as if I were a unique Juliet rose,
Delicately and lovingly.

He looks at me in a way you only see in movies,
Gazes at me in awe and wonder,
Believes in me more than a child's belief that
they can fly with a cape.

He is my person,
My best friend,
And my confidant.

He is my husband.
And though he might debate otherwise,
I am unquestionably the lucky one.

Sometimes the people that are supposed to believe in you are the ones holding you back.

I showed my English professor all my poems
She proposed I take an English major
I showed my mother my best poem
And she called my work "poison," a razor

Cookie Cutter Mold

You pretend to know what I'm feeling,
But how could you when I don't even know
myself.
You tell me I'm talking in circles,
But for the first time in my life, I'm speaking
clearly.

How dare you tell me who I'm supposed to be.
I do not fit in your cookie cutter mold,
Nor do I ever wish to fit.

My perseverance is stronger than your will.
Your perfect, organized world,
Is a pale contrast to my marvel chaos.

The dreams you forbid, I make into reality.
My spirit will not break or bend.
For I, I am a phoenix.

Stuck in Your Mind

Shoot me in the head
Drown me in the sea
Suffocate me in my sleep
But I'll still be there

For the souls that never sleep
And stay awake at night
Till the morning light alarms them
So they shut the blinds

Their thoughts are so dark
That they cut like a knife
But it's actually just me
Waiting to attack

I creep up your back
And nag you in your mind
"Look at how they watch you,"
And I fill you with fright

Your mind shuts down
I have won the fight
Cause forever you'll be stuck
With me, anxiety, in your mind

Interrogating My Consciousness

I feel what others suppress
I feel the pain, hurt, and loss
Among the many things that make love lyrical
And each heartbreak a miracle
I find it ironic
How we think someone can live forever
Even though we all know
That the Grim Reaper is clever
Is it nature?
Or is it love,
That keeps us on our toes?
Until that, that we already know, comes crashing on our door?
How many times can a person be saved?
How many times can one cheat death?
I will ponder these questions,
Until my very last breath.

Thoughts From a Mental Hospital

Sometimes we cry
Without ever knowing why
We ask the universe, "Why am I like this?"
But never get an answer back
Some pray
Some fight
But in the end
We're all the same at night
We feel the emptiness inside us
And the sadness
And the worthlessness
And we can't get those thoughts out of our head
Doctors call it an imbalance of the brain
I call it the effects of life itself
Sometimes it's family that makes us feel this way
And therefore, influence the way we behave

Who Am I?

When I look in the mirror
I have a front-row seat to everything I deem
wrong about myself
But if I were to look at myself through the eyes
of someone who loves me
I would see the incredible person I've become

I am resilient
I am strong
I am beautiful
I am intelligent
I am confident
I am passionate
I am kind
I am trustworthy
I am...

The list is endless
And these are the things you must think about as
you lay in bed at night
Because those negative thoughts are not who
you are
They are merely a filter
When in reality,
You are the light.

www.ingramcontent.com/pod-product-compliance
Lightning Source LLC
Chambersburg PA
CBHW051749130826
49812CB00033B/1075
* 9 7 8 9 3 5 7 2 1 4 4 2 1 *